Book Title	Picture book	Poetry	Fairytale/fable	Myth/legend	Adventure	Non-fiction			
1									
2									
3									
4									
5									
6									
7									
8									
9									
10									
11									
12									
13									
14									
15									
16									
17									
18									
19									
20									
21									
22									
23									
24									
25									

Book Title	Picture book	Poetry	Fairytale/fable	Myth/legend	Adventure	Non-fiction	[Your choice]	[Your choice]	[Your choice]
26									
27									
28									
29									
30									
31									
32									
33									
34									
35									
36									
37									
38									
39									
40									
41									
42									
43									
44									
45									
46									
47									
48									
49									
50									

Book Title	Picture book	Poetry	Fairytale/fable	Myth/legend	Adventure	Non-fiction			
51									
52									
53									
54									
55									
56									
57									
58									
59									
60									
61									
62									
63									
64									
65									
66									
67									
68									
69									
70									
71									
72									
73									
74									
75									

Book Title	Picture book	Poetry	Fairytale/fable	Myth/legend	Adventure	Non-fiction	[Your choice]	[Your choice]	[Your choice]
76									
77									
78									
79									
80									
81									
82									
83									
84									
85									
86									
87									
88									
89									
90									
91									
92									
93									
94									
95									
96									
97									
98									
99									
100									

Paperback ○ Hardback ○ e-book ○ Spoken word ○

Title: The Murmur of Bees

1

COVID19

Dates Started: ~~March~~ April

Finished: April 27th

Source

Bought ○ Loaned ○

From: Kindle prime during Covid

Author: Sofiá Segovia

Cover picture:

Page count:

○ Fiction ○ Non-fiction

Type: Subject:

This was my pick up/put down book so I read several concurrently

My Review:

Loved the book.

Agrarian reform Mexico

1918 pandemic

Life in Mexico peons, landowners

interesting twists

Simonopio

Loved Beatriz

Inspiration Tree

Why I read it?

Intriguing title

Good reviews Free Amazon

It inspired me to (read/learn/visit)?

Who will I recommend it to?

Great lines from this book:

⁎ Ratings ⁎

Plot: 1 2 3 4 5

Characters: 1 2 3 4 5

Ease of reading: 1 2 3 4 5

Overall

2

Paperback ○ Hardback ○ e-book ○ Spoken word ○

Title:

Dates

Started: ____________

Finished: ____________

Source

Bought ○ Loaned ○

From: ____________

Author: ____________

Cover picture: ____________

Page count: ____________

○ Fiction

Type: ____________

○ Non-fiction

Subject: ____________

Inspiration Tree

Why I read it?

____

It inspired me to (read/learn/visit)?

____

____

Who will I recommend it to?

____

My Review: ____________

⁂ Ratings ⁂

Plot: 1 2 3 4 5

Characters: 1 2 3 4 5

Ease of reading: 1 2 3 4 5

Overall

☹ 😐 ☺

Great lines from this book:

Paperback ○ Hardback ○ e-book ○ Spoken word ○

3

Title:

Author: ______

Cover picture: ______

Page count: ______

○ Fiction

Type: ______

○ Non-fiction

Subject: ______

My Review:

Great lines from this book:

Dates

Started: ______

Finished: ______

Source

Bought ○ Loaned ○

From: ______

Inspiration Tree

Why I read it?

______

It inspired me to (read/learn/visit)?

______

______

Who will I recommend it to?

______

⁂ Ratings ⁂

Plot: 1 2 3 4 5

Characters:

1 2 3 4 5

Ease of reading:

1 2 3 4 5

Overall

4

Paperback ○ Hardback ○ e-book ○ Spoken word ○

Title:

Dates

Started: ____________

Finished: __________

Source

Bought ○ Loaned ○

From: ______________

Author: ____________________

Cover picture: ____________________

Page count: ______________

○ Fiction

Type: ______________

○ Non-fiction

Subject: ______________

Inspiration Tree

Why I read it?

____

It inspired me to (read/learn/visit)?

____

____

Who will I recommend it to?

____

My Review: ____________________

* Ratings *

Plot: 1 2 3 4 5

Characters: 1 2 3 4 5

Ease of reading: 1 2 3 4 5

Overall

☹ 😐 ☺

Great lines from this book:

Paperback ○ Hardback ○ e-book ○ Spoken word ○

5

Title:

Author: ______

Cover picture: ______

Page count: ______

○ Fiction
Type: ______

○ Non-fiction
Subject: ______

My Review: ______

Great lines from this book:

Dates

Started: ______

Finished: ______

Source

Bought ○ Loaned ○

From: ______

Inspiration Tree

Why I read it?

______

It inspired me to (read/learn/visit)?

______

______

Who will I recommend it to?

______

⁎ Ratings ⁎

Plot: 1 2 3 4 5

Characters: 1 2 3 4 5

Ease of reading: 1 2 3 4 5

Overall

6

Paperback ○ Hardback ○ e-book ○ Spoken word ○

Title:

Dates
Started: ____________
Finished: ____________

Source
Bought ○ Loaned ○
From: ____________

Author: ____________
Cover picture: ____________
Page count: ____________

○ Fiction
Type: ____________

○ Non-fiction
Subject: ____________

Inspiration Tree

Why I read it?
____

It inspired me to (read/learn/visit)?
____
____

Who will I recommend it to?
____

My Review: ____________

⁎ Ratings ⁎

Plot: 1 2 3 4 5

Characters:
1 2 3 4 5

Ease of reading:
1 2 3 4 5

Overall

☹ 😐 ☺

Great lines from this book:

Paperback ○ Hardback ○ e-book ○ Spoken word ○

7

Title:

Author: ______________________

Cover picture: ______________________

Page count: ______________

○ Fiction
Type: ______________

○ Non-fiction
Subject: ______________

Dates

Started: __________

Finished: __________

Source

Bought ○ Loaned ○

From: __________

My Review: ______________________

Inspiration Tree

Why I read it?

____

It inspired me to (read/learn/visit)?

____

____

Who will I recommend it to?

____

Great lines from this book:

* Ratings *

Plot: 1 2 3 4 5

Characters:
1 2 3 4 5

Ease of reading:
1 2 3 4 5

Overall

8

Paperback ○ Hardback ○ e-book ○ Spoken word ○

Title:

Dates

Started: ____________

Finished: ____________

Source

Bought ○ Loaned ○

From: ____________

Author: ____________

Cover picture: ____________

Page count: ____________

○ Fiction

Type: ____________

○ Non-fiction

Subject: ____________

Inspiration Tree

Why I read it?

____

It inspired me to (read/learn/visit)?

____

____

Who will I recommend it to?

____

My Review: ____________

Ratings

Plot: 1 2 3 4 5

Characters: 1 2 3 4 5

Ease of reading: 1 2 3 4 5

Overall

☹ 😐 ☺

Great lines from this book:

Paperback ○ Hardback ○ e-book ○ Spoken word ○

9

Title:

Author: ______

Cover picture: ______

Page count: ______

○ Fiction
Type: ______

○ Non-fiction
Subject: ______

Dates
Started: ______
Finished: ______

Source
Bought ○ Loaned ○
From: ______

My Review: ______

Inspiration Tree

Why I read it?
______

It inspired me to (read/learn/visit)?
______
______

Who will I recommend it to?
______

Great lines from this book:

✳ Ratings ✳

Plot: 1 2 3 4 5

Characters: 1 2 3 4 5

Ease of reading: 1 2 3 4 5

Overall

10

Paperback ○ Hardback ○ e-book ○ Spoken word ○

Title:

Dates

Started: ____________

Finished: ____________

Source

Bought ○ Loaned ○

From: ____________

Author: ____________

Cover picture: ____________

Page count: ____________

○ Fiction

Type: ____________

○ Non-fiction

Subject: ____________

Inspiration Tree

Why I read it?

____

It inspired me to (read/learn/visit)?

____

____

Who will I recommend it to?

____

My Review: ____________

✻ Ratings ✻

Plot: 1 2 3 4 5

Characters: 1 2 3 4 5

Ease of reading: 1 2 3 4 5

Overall

☹ 😐 ☺

Great lines from this book:

Paperback ○ Hardback ○ e-book ○ Spoken word ○

11

Title:

Author: ______

Cover picture: ______

Page count: ______

○ Fiction
Type: ______

○ Non-fiction
Subject: ______

Dates
Started: ______
Finished: ______

Source
Bought ○ Loaned ○
From: ______

My Review: ______

Inspiration Tree

Why I read it?
______

It inspired me to (read/learn/visit)?
______
______

Who will I recommend it to?
______

Great lines from this book:

⁕ Ratings ⁕

Plot: 1 2 3 4 5

Characters:
1 2 3 4 5

Ease of reading:
1 2 3 4 5

Overall
☹ 😐 ☺

12

Paperback ○ Hardback ○ e-book ○ Spoken word ○

Title:

Author: ____

Cover picture: ____

Page count: ____

○ Fiction
Type: ____

○ Non-fiction
Subject: ____

Dates
Started: ____
Finished: ____

Source
Bought ○ Loaned ○
From: ____

Inspiration Tree

Why I read it?
____

It inspired me to (read/learn/visit)?
____
____

Who will I recommend it to?
____

My Review: ____

⁎ Ratings ⁎

Plot: 1 2 3 4 5

Characters: 1 2 3 4 5

Ease of reading: 1 2 3 4 5

Overall

Great lines from this book:

Paperback ○ Hardback ○ e-book ○ Spoken word ○

13

Title:

Author:

Cover picture:

Page count:

○ Fiction

Type:

○ Non-fiction

Subject:

My Review:

Great lines from this book:

Dates

Started:

Finished:

Source

Bought ○ Loaned ○

From:

Inspiration Tree

Why I read it?

It inspired me to (read/learn/visit)?

Who will I recommend it to?

✳ Ratings ✳

Plot: 1 2 3 4 5

Characters: 1 2 3 4 5

Ease of reading: 1 2 3 4 5

Overall

14

Paperback ○ Hardback ○ e-book ○ Spoken word ○

Title:

Dates

Started: ____________

Finished: ____________

Source

Bought ○ Loaned ○

From: ____________

Author: ____________

Cover picture: ____________

Page count: ____________

○ Fiction

Type: ____________

○ Non-fiction

Subject: ____________

My Review: ____________

Inspiration Tree

Why I read it?

____

It inspired me to (read/learn/visit)?

____

____

Who will I recommend it to?

____

* Ratings *

Plot: 1 2 3 4 5

Characters: 1 2 3 4 5

Ease of reading: 1 2 3 4 5

Overall

Great lines from this book:

Paperback ○ Hardback ○ e-book ○ Spoken word ○

15

Title:

Author:

Cover picture:

Page count:

○ Fiction
Type:

○ Non-fiction
Subject:

Dates
Started:
Finished:

Source
Bought ○ Loaned ○
From:

My Review:

Inspiration Tree

Why I read it?

It inspired me to (read/learn/visit)?

Who will I recommend it to?

Great lines from this book:

⁎ Ratings ⁎

Plot: 1 2 3 4 5

Characters:
1 2 3 4 5

Ease of reading:
1 2 3 4 5

Overall
☹ 😐 ☺

16

Paperback ○ Hardback ○ e-book ○ Spoken word ○

Title:

Dates

Started: ____________

Finished: ____________

Source

Bought ○ Loaned ○

From: ____________

Author: ____________

Cover picture: ____________

Page count: ____________

○ Fiction

Type: ____________

○ Non-fiction

Subject: ____________

Inspiration Tree

Why I read it?

____

It inspired me to (read/learn/visit)?

____

____

Who will I recommend it to?

____

My Review: ____________

✳ Ratings ✳

Plot: 1 2 3 4 5

Characters: 1 2 3 4 5

Ease of reading: 1 2 3 4 5

Overall

☹ 😐 ☺

Great lines from this book:

Paperback ○ Hardback ○ e-book ○ Spoken word ○

17

Title:

Author: ______

Cover picture: ______

Page count: ______

○ Fiction

Type: ______

○ Non-fiction

Subject: ______

My Review: ______

Great lines from this book:

Dates

Started: ______

Finished: ______

Source

Bought ○ Loaned ○

From: ______

Inspiration Tree

Why I read it?

______

It inspired me to (read/learn/visit)?

______

Who will I recommend it to?

______

⁎ Ratings ⁎

Plot: 1 2 3 4 5

Characters: 1 2 3 4 5

Ease of reading: 1 2 3 4 5

Overall

18

Paperback ○ Hardback ○ e-book ○ Spoken word ○

Title:

Dates

Started: ____________

Finished: ____________

Source

Bought ○ Loaned ○

From: ____________

Author: ____________

Cover picture: ____________

Page count: ____________

○ Fiction

Type: ____________

○ Non-fiction

Subject: ____________

My Review: ____________

Inspiration Tree

Why I read it?

It inspired me to (read/learn/visit)?

Who will I recommend it to?

⁕ Ratings ⁕

Plot: 1 2 3 4 5

Characters: 1 2 3 4 5

Ease of reading: 1 2 3 4 5

Overall

☹ 😐 ☺

Great lines from this book:

Paperback ○ Hardback ○ e-book ○ Spoken word ○

19

Title:

Author: ______________________________

Cover picture: ______________________________

Page count: ______________

○ Fiction
Type: ______________

○ Non-fiction
Subject: ______________

Dates
Started: __________
Finished: __________

Source
Bought ○ Loaned ○
From: __________

My Review: ______________________________

Inspiration Tree

Why I read it?

____

It inspired me to (read/learn/visit)?

____

____

Who will I recommend it to?

____

Great lines from this book:

⁕ Ratings ⁕

Plot: 1 2 3 4 5

Characters:
1 2 3 4 5

Ease of reading:
1 2 3 4 5

Overall

20

Paperback ○ Hardback ○ e-book ○ Spoken word ○

Title:

Dates

Started: ____________

Finished: ____________

Source

Bought ○ Loaned ○

From: ____________

Author: ____________

Cover picture: ____________

Page count: ____________

○ Fiction

Type: ____________

○ Non-fiction

Subject: ____________

Inspiration Tree

Why I read it?

____

It inspired me to (read/learn/visit)?

____

____

Who will I recommend it to?

____

My Review: ____________

* Ratings *

Plot: 1 2 3 4 5

Characters: 1 2 3 4 5

Ease of reading: 1 2 3 4 5

Overall

Great lines from this book:

Paperback ○ Hardback ○ e-book ○ Spoken word ○

21

Title:

Author:

Cover picture:

Page count:

○ Fiction
Type:

○ Non-fiction
Subject:

Dates
Started:
Finished:

Source
Bought ○ Loaned ○
From:

My Review:

Inspiration Tree

Why I read it?

It inspired me to (read/learn/visit)?

Who will I recommend it to?

Great lines from this book:

✳ Ratings ✳

Plot: 1 2 3 4 5

Characters: 1 2 3 4 5

Ease of reading: 1 2 3 4 5

Overall
☹ 😐 ☺

22

Paperback ○ Hardback ○ e-book ○ Spoken word ○

Title:

Dates

Started: ____________

Finished: ____________

Source

Bought ○ Loaned ○

From: ____________

Author: ____________

Cover picture: ____________

Page count: ____________

○ Fiction

Type: ____________

○ Non-fiction

Subject: ____________

Inspiration Tree

Why I read it?

____

It inspired me to (read/learn/visit)?

____

Who will I recommend it to?

____

My Review: ____________

✳ Ratings ✳

Plot: 1 2 3 4 5

Characters: 1 2 3 4 5

Ease of reading: 1 2 3 4 5

Overall

Great lines from this book:

Paperback ○ Hardback ○ e-book ○ Spoken word ○

Title:

23

Author:

Cover picture:

Page count:

○ Fiction

Type:

○ Non-fiction

Subject:

My Review:

Great lines from this book:

Dates

Started:

Finished:

Source

Bought ○ Loaned ○

From:

Inspiration Tree

Why I read it?

It inspired me to (read/learn/visit)?

Who will I recommend it to?

⁂ Ratings ⁂

Plot: 1 2 3 4 5

Characters: 1 2 3 4 5

Ease of reading: 1 2 3 4 5

Overall

24

Paperback ○ Hardback ○ e-book ○ Spoken word ○

Title:

Dates

Started: ____________

Finished: ____________

Source

Bought ○ Loaned ○

From: ____________

Author: ____________

Cover picture: ____________

Page count: ____________

○ Fiction

Type: ____________

○ Non-fiction

Subject: ____________

My Review: ____________

Inspiration Tree

Why I read it?

____

It inspired me to (read/learn/visit)?

____

____

Who will I recommend it to?

____

⁂ Ratings ⁂

Plot: 1 2 3 4 5

Characters:

1 2 3 4 5

Ease of reading:

1 2 3 4 5

Overall

☹ 😐 ☺

Great lines from this book:

Paperback ○ Hardback ○ e-book ○ Spoken word ○

25

Title:

Author: ______

Cover picture: ______

Page count: ______

○ Fiction
Type: ______

○ Non-fiction
Subject: ______

Dates

Started: ______

Finished: ______

Source

Bought ○ Loaned ○

From: ______

My Review: ______

Inspiration Tree

Why I read it?

______

It inspired me to (read/learn/visit)?

______

______

Who will I recommend it to?

______

✳ Ratings ✳

Plot: 1 2 3 4 5

Characters: 1 2 3 4 5

Ease of reading: 1 2 3 4 5

Overall

Great lines from this book:

26

Paperback ○ Hardback ○ e-book ○ Spoken word ○

Title:

Dates

Started: ____________

Finished: ____________

Source

Bought ○ Loaned ○

From: ____________

Author: ____________

Cover picture: ____________

Page count: ____________

○ Fiction

Type: ____________

○ Non-fiction

Subject: ____________

My Review: ____________

Inspiration Tree

Why I read it?

____

It inspired me to (read/learn/visit)?

____

____

Who will I recommend it to?

____

⁎ Ratings ⁎

Plot: 1 2 3 4 5

Characters: 1 2 3 4 5

Ease of reading: 1 2 3 4 5

Overall

☹ 😐 ☺

Great lines from this book:

Paperback ○ Hardback ○ e-book ○ Spoken word ○

27

Title:

Author:

Cover picture:

Page count:

○ Fiction

Type:

○ Non-fiction

Subject:

Dates

Started:

Finished:

Source

Bought ○ Loaned ○

From:

My Review:

Inspiration Tree

Why I read it?

It inspired me to (read/learn/visit)?

Who will I recommend it to?

Great lines from this book:

⁕ Ratings ⁕

Plot: 1 2 3 4 5

Characters: 1 2 3 4 5

Ease of reading: 1 2 3 4 5

Overall

28

Paperback ○ Hardback ○ e-book ○ Spoken word ○

Title:

Dates

Started: ____________

Finished: ____________

Source

Bought ○ Loaned ○

From: ____________

Author: ____________

Cover picture: ____________

Page count: ____________

○ Fiction

Type: ____________

○ Non-fiction

Subject: ____________

Inspiration Tree

Why I read it?

It inspired me to (read/learn/visit)?

Who will I recommend it to?

My Review:

⁂ Ratings ⁂

Plot: 1 2 3 4 5

Characters: 1 2 3 4 5

Ease of reading: 1 2 3 4 5

Overall

Great lines from this book:

Paperback ○ Hardback ○ e-book ○ Spoken word ○

29

Title:

Author: ______________________

Cover picture: ______________________

Page count: ______________

○ Fiction

Type: ______________

○ Non-fiction

Subject: ______________

My Review: ______________________

Great lines from this book:

Dates

Started: ______________

Finished: ______________

Source

Bought ○ Loaned ○

From: ______________

Inspiration Tree

Why I read it?

____

It inspired me to (read/learn/visit)?

____

____

Who will I recommend it to?

____

✱ Ratings ✱

Plot: 1 2 3 4 5

Characters:
1 2 3 4 5

Ease of reading:
1 2 3 4 5

Overall

30

Paperback ○ Hardback ○ e-book ○ Spoken word ○

Title:

Dates

Started: ___________

Finished: _________

Source

Bought ○ Loaned ○

From: ____________

Author: ______________________________

Cover picture: ______________________________

Page count: ____________

○ Fiction

Type: ______________

○ Non-fiction

Subject: ____________

My Review: ______________________________

Inspiration Tree

Why I read it?

____

It inspired me to (read/learn/visit)?

____

____

Who will I recommend it to?

____

✱ Ratings ✱

Plot: 1 2 3 4 5

Characters: 1 2 3 4 5

Ease of reading: 1 2 3 4 5

Overall

Great lines from this book:

Paperback ○ Hardback ○ e-book ○ Spoken word ○

Title:

31

Author:

Cover picture:

Page count:

○ Fiction

Type:

○ Non-fiction

Subject:

Dates

Started:

Finished:

Source

Bought ○ Loaned ○

From:

My Review:

Inspiration Tree

Why I read it?

It inspired me to (read/learn/visit)?

Who will I recommend it to?

Great lines from this book:

Ratings

Plot: 1 2 3 4 5

Characters: 1 2 3 4 5

Ease of reading: 1 2 3 4 5

Overall

32

Paperback ○ Hardback ○ e-book ○ Spoken word ○

Title:

Dates

Started: ____________

Finished: ____________

Source

Bought ○ Loaned ○

From: ____________

Author: ____________

Cover picture: ____________

Page count: ____________

○ Fiction

Type: ____________

○ Non-fiction

Subject: ____________

My Review: ____________

Inspiration Tree

Why I read it?

____

It inspired me to (read/learn/visit)?

____

____

Who will I recommend it to?

____

✳ Ratings ✳

Plot: 1 2 3 4 5

Characters: 1 2 3 4 5

Ease of reading: 1 2 3 4 5

Overall

☹ 😐 ☺

Great lines from this book:

Paperback ○ Hardback ○ e-book ○ Spoken word ○

Title:

33

Author:

Cover picture:

Page count:

○ Fiction

Type:

○ Non-fiction

Subject:

Dates

Started:

Finished:

Source

Bought ○ Loaned ○

From:

My Review:

Inspiration Tree

Why I read it?

It inspired me to (read/learn/visit)?

Who will I recommend it to?

Great lines from this book:

⁕ Ratings ⁕

Plot: 1 2 3 4 5

Characters: 1 2 3 4 5

Ease of reading: 1 2 3 4 5

Overall

34

Paperback ○ Hardback ○ e-book ○ Spoken word ○

Title:

Author:

Cover picture:

Page count:

○ Fiction

Type:

○ Non-fiction

Subject:

Dates

Started:

Finished:

Source

Bought ○ Loaned ○

From:

My Review:

Inspiration Tree

Why I read it?

It inspired me to (read/learn/visit)?

Who will I recommend it to?

✳ Ratings ✳

Plot: 1 2 3 4 5

Characters: 1 2 3 4 5

Ease of reading: 1 2 3 4 5

Overall

Great lines from this book:

Paperback ○ Hardback ○ e-book ○ Spoken word ○

Title:

35

Author:

Cover picture:

Page count:

○ Fiction

Type:

○ Non-fiction

Subject:

Dates

Started:

Finished:

Source

Bought ○ Loaned ○

From:

My Review:

Inspiration Tree

Why I read it?

It inspired me to (read/learn/visit)?

Who will I recommend it to?

Great lines from this book:

⁂ Ratings ⁂

Plot: 1 2 3 4 5

Characters: 1 2 3 4 5

Ease of reading: 1 2 3 4 5

Overall

36

Paperback ○ Hardback ○ e-book ○ Spoken word ○

Title:

Dates

Started: ____________

Finished: ____________

Source

Bought ○ Loaned ○

From: ____________

Author: ____________

Cover picture: ____________

Page count: ____________

○ Fiction

Type: ____________

○ Non-fiction

Subject: ____________

My Review: ____________

Inspiration Tree

Why I read it?

____

It inspired me to (read/learn/visit)?

____

____

Who will I recommend it to?

____

⚹ Ratings ⚹

Plot: 1 2 3 4 5

Characters: 1 2 3 4 5

Ease of reading: 1 2 3 4 5

Overall

☹ 😐 ☺

Great lines from this book:

Paperback ○ Hardback ○ e-book ○ Spoken word ○

Title:

37

Author:

Cover picture:

Page count:

○ Fiction

Type:

○ Non-fiction

Subject:

Dates

Started:

Finished:

Source

Bought ○ Loaned ○

From:

My Review:

Inspiration Tree

Why I read it?

It inspired me to (read/learn/visit)?

Who will I recommend it to?

Great lines from this book:

✳ Ratings ✳

Plot: 1 2 3 4 5

Characters: 1 2 3 4 5

Ease of reading: 1 2 3 4 5

Overall

☹ 😐 ☺

38

Paperback ○ Hardback ○ e-book ○ Spoken word ○

Title:

Dates

Started: ___________

Finished: _________

Source

Bought ○ Loaned ○

From: ____________

Inspiration Tree

Why I read it?

____

It inspired me to (read/learn/visit)?

____

____

Who will I recommend it to?

____

✻ Ratings ✻

Plot: 1 2 3 4 5

Characters: 1 2 3 4 5

Ease of reading: 1 2 3 4 5

Overall

☹ 😐 ☺

Author: ____________________

Cover picture: ____________________

Page count: ____________

○ Fiction

Type: ____________

○ Non-fiction

Subject: ____________

My Review: ____________________

Great lines from this book:

Paperback ○ Hardback ○ e-book ○ Spoken word ○

Title:

39

Author:

Cover picture:

Page count:

○ Fiction

Type:

○ Non-fiction

Subject:

Dates

Started:

Finished:

Source

Bought ○ Loaned ○

From:

My Review:

Inspiration Tree

Why I read it?

It inspired me to (read/learn/visit)?

Who will I recommend it to?

⁎ Ratings ⁎

Plot: 1 2 3 4 5

Characters: 1 2 3 4 5

Ease of reading: 1 2 3 4 5

Overall

Great lines from this book:

40

Paperback ○ Hardback ○ e-book ○ Spoken word ○

Title:

Dates

Started: ____________

Finished: ____________

Source

Bought ○ Loaned ○

From: ____________

Author: ____________

Cover picture: ____________

Page count: ____________

○ Fiction

Type: ____________

○ Non-fiction

Subject: ____________

Inspiration Tree

Why I read it?

____

It inspired me to (read/learn/visit)?

____

____

Who will I recommend it to?

____

My Review:

____

⁎ Ratings ⁎

Plot: 1 2 3 4 5

Characters:
1 2 3 4 5

Ease of reading:
1 2 3 4 5

Overall

Great lines from this book:

Paperback ○ Hardback ○ e-book ○ Spoken word ○

41

Title:

Author: ______________________

Cover picture: ______________________

Page count: __________

○ Fiction

Type: __________

○ Non-fiction

Subject: __________

My Review: ______________________

Great lines from this book:

Dates

Started: __________

Finished: __________

Source

Bought ○ Loaned ○

From: __________

Inspiration Tree

Why I read it?

____

It inspired me to (read/learn/visit)?

____

____

Who will I recommend it to?

____

✳ Ratings ✳

Plot: 1 2 3 4 5

Characters:

1 2 3 4 5

Ease of reading:

1 2 3 4 5

Overall

42

Paperback ○ Hardback ○ e-book ○ Spoken word ○

Title:

Dates

Started: ____________

Finished: ____________

Source

Bought ○ Loaned ○

From: ____________

Author: ____________

Cover picture: ____________

Page count: ____________

○ Fiction

Type: ____________

○ Non-fiction

Subject: ____________

My Review: ____________

Inspiration Tree

Why I read it?

____

It inspired me to (read/learn/visit)?

____

____

Who will I recommend it to?

____

⁂ Ratings ⁂

Plot: 1 2 3 4 5

Characters: 1 2 3 4 5

Ease of reading: 1 2 3 4 5

Overall

☹ 😐 ☺

Great lines from this book:

Paperback ○ Hardback ○ e-book ○ Spoken word ○

43

Title:

Author: __________

Cover picture: __________

Page count: __________

○ Fiction
Type: __________

○ Non-fiction
Subject: __________

Dates
Started: __________
Finished: __________

Source
Bought ○ Loaned ○
From: __________

My Review: __________

Inspiration Tree

Why I read it?

____

It inspired me to (read/learn/visit)?

____

Who will I recommend it to?

____

Great lines from this book:

⁎ Ratings ⁎

Plot: 1 2 3 4 5

Characters: 1 2 3 4 5

Ease of reading: 1 2 3 4 5

Overall

44

Paperback ○ Hardback ○ e-book ○ Spoken word ○

Title:

Dates

Started: ____________

Finished: ____________

Source

Bought ○ Loaned ○

From: ____________

Author: ____________

Cover picture: ____________

Page count: ____________

○ Fiction

Type: ____________

○ Non-fiction

Subject: ____________

Inspiration Tree

Why I read it?

____

It inspired me to (read/learn/visit)?

____

____

Who will I recommend it to?

____

My Review: ____________

✻ Ratings ✻

Plot: 1 2 3 4 5

Characters: 1 2 3 4 5

Ease of reading: 1 2 3 4 5

Overall

☹ 😐 ☺

Great lines from this book:

Paperback ○ Hardback ○ e-book ○ Spoken word ○

45

Title:

Author: ____________________

Cover picture: ____________________

Page count: ____________

○ Fiction
Type: ____________

○ Non-fiction
Subject: ____________

My Review: ____________________

Great lines from this book:

Dates

Started: ____________

Finished: ____________

Source

Bought ○ Loaned ○

From: ____________

Inspiration Tree

Why I read it?

____

It inspired me to (read/learn/visit)?

____

____

Who will I recommend it to?

____

⁎ Ratings ⁎

Plot: 1 2 3 4 5

Characters: 1 2 3 4 5

Ease of reading: 1 2 3 4 5

Overall

46

Paperback ○ Hardback ○ e-book ○ Spoken word ○

Title:

Dates

Started: ___________

Finished: ___________

Source

Bought ○ Loaned ○

From: ___________

Author: ___________

Cover picture: ___________

Page count: ___________

○ Fiction

Type: ___________

○ Non-fiction

Subject: ___________

Inspiration Tree

Why I read it?

____

It inspired me to (read/learn/visit)?

____

____

Who will I recommend it to?

____

My Review: ___________

* Ratings *

Plot: 1 2 3 4 5

Characters: 1 2 3 4 5

Ease of reading: 1 2 3 4 5

Overall

☹ 😐 ☺

Great lines from this book:

Paperback ○ Hardback ○ e-book ○ Spoken word ○

47

Title:

Author: ____

Cover picture: ____

Page count: ____

○ Fiction
Type: ____

○ Non-fiction
Subject: ____

Dates
Started: ____
Finished: ____

Source
Bought ○ Loaned ○
From: ____

My Review: ____

Inspiration Tree

Why I read it?
____
It inspired me to (read/learn/visit)?
____
Who will I recommend it to?
____

Great lines from this book:

⁎ Ratings ⁎

Plot: 1 2 3 4 5
Characters: 1 2 3 4 5
Ease of reading: 1 2 3 4 5
Overall
☹ 😐 ☺

48

Paperback ○ Hardback ○ e-book ○ Spoken word ○

Title:

Dates

Started: ____________

Finished: ____________

Source

Bought ○ Loaned ○

From: ____________

Author: ____________

Cover picture: ____________

Page count: ____________

○ Fiction

Type: ____________

○ Non-fiction

Subject: ____________

My Review: ____________

Inspiration Tree

Why I read it?

↓

It inspired me to (read/learn/visit)?

↓

Who will I recommend it to?

✳ Ratings ✳

Plot: 1 2 3 4 5

Characters: 1 2 3 4 5

Ease of reading: 1 2 3 4 5

Overall

☹ 😐 ☺

Great lines from this book:

Paperback ○ Hardback ○ e-book ○ Spoken word ○

49

Title:

Author:

Cover picture:

Page count:

○ Fiction

Type:

○ Non-fiction

Subject:

Dates

Started:

Finished:

Source

Bought ○ Loaned ○

From:

My Review:

Inspiration Tree

Why I read it?

It inspired me to (read/learn/visit)?

Who will I recommend it to?

✱ Ratings ✱

Plot: 1 2 3 4 5

Characters: 1 2 3 4 5

Ease of reading: 1 2 3 4 5

Overall

Great lines from this book:

50

Paperback ○ Hardback ○ e-book ○ Spoken word ○

Title:

Dates

Started: ____________

Finished: __________

Source

Bought ○ Loaned ○

From: ____________

Author: ______________________________

Cover picture: ______________________________

Page count: ____________

○ Fiction

Type: ____________

○ Non-fiction

Subject: ____________

Inspiration Tree

Why I read it?

____

It inspired me to (read/learn/visit)?

____

____

Who will I recommend it to?

____

My Review: ______________________________

✳ Ratings ✳

Plot: 1 2 3 4 5

Characters: 1 2 3 4 5

Ease of reading: 1 2 3 4 5

Overall

Great lines from this book:

Paperback ○ Hardback ○ e-book ○ Spoken word ○

Title:

51

Author:

Cover picture:

Page count:

○ Fiction

Type:

○ Non-fiction

Subject:

Dates

Started:

Finished:

Source

Bought ○ Loaned ○

From:

My Review:

Inspiration Tree

Why I read it?

It inspired me to (read/learn/visit)?

Who will I recommend it to?

Great lines from this book:

⁂ Ratings ⁂

Plot: 1 2 3 4 5

Characters: 1 2 3 4 5

Ease of reading: 1 2 3 4 5

Overall

52

Paperback ○ Hardback ○ e-book ○ Spoken word ○

Title:

Dates

Started: ____________

Finished: ____________

Source

Bought ○ Loaned ○

From: ____________

Author: ____________

Cover picture: ____________

Page count: ____________

○ Fiction

Type: ____________

○ Non-fiction

Subject: ____________

My Review: ____________

Inspiration Tree

Why I read it?

____

It inspired me to (read/learn/visit)?

____

____

Who will I recommend it to?

____

* Ratings *

Plot: 1 2 3 4 5

Characters: 1 2 3 4 5

Ease of reading: 1 2 3 4 5

Overall

Great lines from this book:

Paperback ○ Hardback ○ e-book ○ Spoken word ○

53

Title:

Author: ______

Cover picture: ______

Page count: ______

○ Fiction
Type: ______

○ Non-fiction
Subject: ______

Dates

Started: ______

Finished: ______

Source

Bought ○ Loaned ○

From: ______

My Review: ______

Inspiration Tree

Why I read it?

______

It inspired me to (read/learn/visit)?

______

Who will I recommend it to?

______

Great lines from this book:

✳ Ratings ✳

Plot: 1 2 3 4 5

Characters: 1 2 3 4 5

Ease of reading: 1 2 3 4 5

Overall

54

Paperback ○ Hardback ○ e-book ○ Spoken word ○

Title:

Dates

Started: ____________

Finished: ____________

Source

Bought ○ Loaned ○

From: ____________

Author: ____________

Cover picture: ____________

Page count: ____________

○ Fiction

Type: ____________

○ Non-fiction

Subject: ____________

Inspiration Tree

Why I read it?

____

It inspired me to (read/learn/visit)?

____

____

Who will I recommend it to?

____

My Review: ____________

✳ Ratings ✳

Plot: 1 2 3 4 5

Characters: 1 2 3 4 5

Ease of reading: 1 2 3 4 5

Overall

☹ 😐 ☺

Great lines from this book:

Paperback ○ Hardback ○ e-book ○ Spoken word ○

55

Title:

Author:

Cover picture:

Page count:

○ Fiction

Type:

○ Non-fiction

Subject:

Dates

Started:

Finished:

Source

Bought ○ Loaned ○

From:

My Review:

Inspiration Tree

Why I read it?

It inspired me to (read/learn/visit)?

Who will I recommend it to?

✱ Ratings ✱

Plot: 1 2 3 4 5

Characters: 1 2 3 4 5

Ease of reading: 1 2 3 4 5

Overall

☹ 😐 ☺

Great lines from this book:

56

Paperback ○ Hardback ○ e-book ○ Spoken word ○

Title:

Dates

Started: ____________

Finished: ____________

Source

Bought ○ Loaned ○

From: ____________

Author: ____________

Cover picture: ____________

Page count: ____________

○ Fiction

Type: ____________

○ Non-fiction

Subject: ____________

My Review: ____________

Inspiration Tree

Why I read it?

____

It inspired me to (read/learn/visit)?

____

____

Who will I recommend it to?

____

⁕ Ratings ⁕

Plot: 1 2 3 4 5

Characters:

1 2 3 4 5

Ease of reading:

1 2 3 4 5

Overall

Great lines from this book:

Paperback ○ Hardback ○ e-book ○ Spoken word ○

57

Title:

Author: __________

Cover picture: __________

Page count: __________

○ Fiction

Type: __________

○ Non-fiction

Subject: __________

My Review: __________

Great lines from this book:

Dates

Started: __________

Finished: __________

Source

Bought ○ Loaned ○

From: __________

Inspiration Tree

Why I read it?

____

It inspired me to (read/learn/visit)?

____

Who will I recommend it to?

____

⁕ Ratings ⁕

Plot: 1 2 3 4 5

Characters: 1 2 3 4 5

Ease of reading: 1 2 3 4 5

Overall

58

Paperback ○ Hardback ○ e-book ○ Spoken word ○

Title:

Dates

Started: ____________

Finished: ____________

Source

Bought ○ Loaned ○

From: ____________

Author: ____________

Cover picture: ____________

Page count: ____________

○ Fiction

Type: ____________

○ Non-fiction

Subject: ____________

Inspiration Tree

Why I read it?

____

It inspired me to (read/learn/visit)?

____

____

Who will I recommend it to?

____

My Review: ____________

* Ratings *

Plot: 1 2 3 4 5

Characters: 1 2 3 4 5

Ease of reading: 1 2 3 4 5

Overall

Great lines from this book:

Paperback ○ Hardback ○ e-book ○ Spoken word ○

59

Title:

Author:

Cover picture:

Page count:

○ Fiction

Type:

○ Non-fiction

Subject:

My Review:

Great lines from this book:

Dates

Started:

Finished:

Source

Bought ○ Loaned ○

From:

Inspiration Tree

Why I read it?

It inspired me to (read/learn/visit)?

Who will I recommend it to?

⁎ Ratings ⁎

Plot: 1 2 3 4 5

Characters: 1 2 3 4 5

Ease of reading: 1 2 3 4 5

Overall

60

Paperback ○ Hardback ○ e-book ○ Spoken word ○

Title:

Dates

Started: ____________

Finished: ____________

Source

Bought ○ Loaned ○

From: ____________

Author: ____________

Cover picture: ____________

Page count: ____________

○ Fiction

Type: ____________

○ Non-fiction

Subject: ____________

My Review: ____________

Inspiration Tree

Why I read it?

It inspired me to (read/learn/visit)?

Who will I recommend it to?

* Ratings *

Plot: 1 2 3 4 5

Characters: 1 2 3 4 5

Ease of reading: 1 2 3 4 5

Overall

Great lines from this book:

Paperback ○ Hardback ○ e-book ○ Spoken word ○

61

Title:

Author:

Cover picture:

Page count:

○ Fiction

Type:

○ Non-fiction

Subject:

Dates

Started:

Finished:

Source

Bought ○ Loaned ○

From:

My Review:

Inspiration Tree

Why I read it?

It inspired me to (read/learn/visit)?

Who will I recommend it to?

Great lines from this book:

Ratings

Plot: 1 2 3 4 5

Characters: 1 2 3 4 5

Ease of reading: 1 2 3 4 5

Overall

62

Paperback ○ Hardback ○ e-book ○ Spoken word ○

Title:

Dates

Started: __________

Finished: __________

Source

Bought ○ Loaned ○

From: __________

Author: __________

Cover picture: __________

Page count: __________

○ Fiction

Type: __________

○ Non-fiction

Subject: __________

My Review: __________

Inspiration Tree

Why I read it?

It inspired me to (read/learn/visit)?

Who will I recommend it to?

⁂ Ratings ⁂

Plot: 1 2 3 4 5

Characters:

1 2 3 4 5

Ease of reading:

1 2 3 4 5

Overall

☹ 😐 ☺

Great lines from this book:

Paperback ○ Hardback ○ e-book ○ Spoken word ○

63

Title:

Author: ____________________

Cover picture: ____________________

Page count: __________

○ Fiction

Type: __________

○ Non-fiction

Subject: __________

My Review: ____________________

Great lines from this book:

Dates

Started: __________

Finished: __________

Source

Bought ○ Loaned ○

From: __________

Inspiration Tree

Why I read it?

____

It inspired me to (read/learn/visit)?

____

____

Who will I recommend it to?

____

⁂ Ratings ⁂

Plot: 1 2 3 4 5

Characters: 1 2 3 4 5

Ease of reading: 1 2 3 4 5

Overall

☹ 😐 ☺

64

Paperback ○ Hardback ○ e-book ○ Spoken word ○

Title:

Dates

Started: ____________

Finished: ____________

Source

Bought ○ Loaned ○

From: ____________

Author: ____________

Cover picture: ____________

Page count: ____________

○ Fiction

Type: ____________

○ Non-fiction

Subject: ____________

Inspiration Tree

Why I read it?

____

It inspired me to (read/learn/visit)?

____

____

Who will I recommend it to?

____

My Review: ____________

✳ Ratings ✳

Plot: 1 2 3 4 5

Characters: 1 2 3 4 5

Ease of reading: 1 2 3 4 5

Overall

☹ 😐 ☺

Great lines from this book:

Paperback ○ Hardback ○ e-book ○ Spoken word ○

65

Title:

Author:

Cover picture:

Page count:

○ Fiction
Type:

○ Non-fiction
Subject:

Dates

Started:

Finished:

Source

Bought ○ Loaned ○

From:

My Review:

Great lines from this book:

Inspiration Tree

Why I read it?

It inspired me to (read/learn/visit)?

Who will I recommend it to?

✳ Ratings ✳

Plot: 1 2 3 4 5

Characters: 1 2 3 4 5

Ease of reading: 1 2 3 4 5

Overall

66

Paperback ○ Hardback ○ e-book ○ Spoken word ○

Title:

Dates

Started: ____________

Finished: ____________

Source

Bought ○ Loaned ○

From: ____________

Author: ____________

Cover picture: ____________

Page count: ____________

○ Fiction

Type: ____________

○ Non-fiction

Subject: ____________

My Review: ____________

Inspiration Tree

Why I read it?

____

It inspired me to (read/learn/visit)?

____

Who will I recommend it to?

____

⁎ Ratings ⁎

Plot: 1 2 3 4 5

Characters:

1 2 3 4 5

Ease of reading:

1 2 3 4 5

Overall

☹ 😐 ☺

Great lines from this book:

Paperback ○ Hardback ○ e-book ○ Spoken word ○

67

Title:

Author:

Cover picture:

Page count:

○ Fiction

Type:

○ Non-fiction

Subject:

Dates

Started:

Finished:

Source

Bought ○ Loaned ○

From:

My Review:

Inspiration Tree

Why I read it?

It inspired me to (read/learn/visit)?

Who will I recommend it to?

⁎ Ratings ⁎

Plot: 1 2 3 4 5

Characters:

1 2 3 4 5

Ease of reading:

1 2 3 4 5

Overall

Great lines from this book:

68

Paperback ○ Hardback ○ e-book ○ Spoken word ○

Title:

Dates

Started: ____________

Finished: ____________

Source

Bought ○ Loaned ○

From: ____________

Author: ____________

Cover picture: ____________

Page count: ____________

○ Fiction

Type: ____________

○ Non-fiction

Subject: ____________

Inspiration Tree

Why I read it?

____

It inspired me to (read/learn/visit)?

____

____

Who will I recommend it to?

____

My Review: ____________

✳ Ratings ✳

Plot: 1 2 3 4 5

Characters: 1 2 3 4 5

Ease of reading: 1 2 3 4 5

Overall

☹ 😐 ☺

Great lines from this book:

Paperback ○ Hardback ○ e-book ○ Spoken word ○

69

Title:

Author: ______

Cover picture: ______

Page count: ______

○ Fiction
Type: ______

○ Non-fiction
Subject: ______

Dates
Started: ______
Finished: ______

Source
Bought ○ Loaned ○
From: ______

My Review: ______

Inspiration Tree

Why I read it?
______

It inspired me to (read/learn/visit)?
______

Who will I recommend it to?
______

Great lines from this book:

⁂ Ratings ⁂

Plot: 1 2 3 4 5

Characters:
1 2 3 4 5

Ease of reading:
1 2 3 4 5

Overall

70

Paperback ○ Hardback ○ e-book ○ Spoken word ○

Title:

Dates

Started: ____________

Finished: __________

Source

Bought ○ Loaned ○

From: ______________

Author: ____________

Cover picture: ____________

Page count: ____________

○ Fiction

Type: ____________

○ Non-fiction

Subject: ____________

Inspiration Tree

Why I read it?

____

It inspired me to (read/learn/visit)?

____

____

Who will I recommend it to?

____

My Review: ____________

⁂ Ratings ⁂

Plot: 1 2 3 4 5

Characters: 1 2 3 4 5

Ease of reading: 1 2 3 4 5

Overall

☹ 😐 ☺

Great lines from this book:

Paperback ○ Hardback ○ e-book ○ Spoken word ○

Title:

71

Author: ______

Cover picture: ______

Page count: ______

○ Fiction
Type: ______

○ Non-fiction
Subject: ______

Dates
Started: ______
Finished: ______

Source
Bought ○ Loaned ○
From: ______

My Review: ______

Inspiration Tree

Why I read it?
______

It inspired me to (read/learn/visit)?
______

Who will I recommend it to?
______

Great lines from this book:

⁎ Ratings ⁎

Plot: 1 2 3 4 5

Characters:
1 2 3 4 5

Ease of reading:
1 2 3 4 5

Overall

72

Paperback ○ Hardback ○ e-book ○ Spoken word ○

Title:

Dates

Started: ____________

Finished: ____________

Source

Bought ○ Loaned ○

From: ____________

Author: ____________

Cover picture: ____________

Page count: ____________

○ Fiction

Type: ____________

○ Non-fiction

Subject: ____________

Inspiration Tree

Why I read it?

____

It inspired me to (read/learn/visit)?

____

____

Who will I recommend it to?

____

My Review: ____________

✳ Ratings ✳

Plot: 1 2 3 4 5

Characters:

1 2 3 4 5

Ease of reading:

1 2 3 4 5

Overall

☹ 😐 ☺

Great lines from this book:

Paperback ○ Hardback ○ e-book ○ Spoken word ○

73

Title:

Author:

Cover picture:

Page count:

○ Fiction

Type:

○ Non-fiction

Subject:

My Review:

Great lines from this book:

Dates

Started:

Finished:

Source

Bought ○ Loaned ○

From:

Inspiration Tree

Why I read it?

It inspired me to (read/learn/visit)?

Who will I recommend it to?

✳ Ratings ✳

Plot: 1 2 3 4 5

Characters: 1 2 3 4 5

Ease of reading: 1 2 3 4 5

Overall

74

Paperback ○ Hardback ○ e-book ○ Spoken word ○

Title:

Dates

Started: ____________

Finished: ____________

Source

Bought ○ Loaned ○

From: ____________

Author: ____________

Cover picture: ____________

Page count: ____________

○ Fiction

Type: ____________

○ Non-fiction

Subject: ____________

My Review: ____________

Inspiration Tree

Why I read it?

____

It inspired me to (read/learn/visit)?

____

____

Who will I recommend it to?

____

⁕ Ratings ⁕

Plot: 1 2 3 4 5

Characters: 1 2 3 4 5

Ease of reading: 1 2 3 4 5

Overall

Great lines from this book:

Paperback ○ Hardback ○ e-book ○ Spoken word ○

75

Title:

Author:

Cover picture:

Page count:

○ Fiction
Type:

○ Non-fiction
Subject:

My Review:

Great lines from this book:

Dates
Started:
Finished:

Source
Bought ○ Loaned ○
From:

Inspiration Tree

Why I read it?

It inspired me to (read/learn/visit)?

Who will I recommend it to?

⁕ Ratings ⁕

Plot: 1 2 3 4 5

Characters:
1 2 3 4 5

Ease of reading:
1 2 3 4 5

Overall

76

Paperback ○ Hardback ○ e-book ○ Spoken word ○

Title:

Dates

Started: ____________

Finished: ____________

Source

Bought ○ Loaned ○

From: ____________

Author: ____________

Cover picture: ____________

Page count: ____________

○ Fiction

Type: ____________

○ Non-fiction

Subject: ____________

Inspiration Tree

Why I read it?

____

It inspired me to (read/learn/visit)?

____

____

Who will I recommend it to?

____

My Review: ____________

✳ Ratings ✳

Plot: 1 2 3 4 5

Characters: 1 2 3 4 5

Ease of reading: 1 2 3 4 5

Overall

☹ 😐 ☺

Great lines from this book:

Paperback ○ Hardback ○ e-book ○ Spoken word ○

77

Title:

Author: ______

Cover picture: ______

Page count: ______

○ Fiction

Type: ______

○ Non-fiction

Subject: ______

My Review: ______

Great lines from this book:

Dates

Started: ______

Finished: ______

Source

Bought ○ Loaned ○

From: ______

Inspiration Tree

Why I read it?

______

It inspired me to (read/learn/visit)?

______

______

Who will I recommend it to?

______

✱ Ratings ✱

Plot: 1 2 3 4 5

Characters:

1 2 3 4 5

Ease of reading:

1 2 3 4 5

Overall

☹ 😐 ☺

78

Paperback ○ Hardback ○ e-book ○ Spoken word ○

Title:

Dates

Started: ____________

Finished: ____________

Source

Bought ○ Loaned ○

From: ____________

Author: ____________

Cover picture: ____________

Page count: ____________

○ Fiction

Type: ____________

○ Non-fiction

Subject: ____________

My Review: ____________

Inspiration Tree

Why I read it?

____

It inspired me to (read/learn/visit)?

____

____

Who will I recommend it to?

____

⁕ Ratings ⁕

Plot: 1 2 3 4 5

Characters:

1 2 3 4 5

Ease of reading:

1 2 3 4 5

Overall

☹ 😐 ☺

Great lines from this book:

Paperback ○ Hardback ○ e-book ○ Spoken word ○

79

Title:

Author:

Cover picture:

Page count:

○ Fiction

Type:

○ Non-fiction

Subject:

Dates

Started:

Finished:

Source

Bought ○ Loaned ○

From:

My Review:

Inspiration Tree

Why I read it?

It inspired me to (read/learn/visit)?

Who will I recommend it to?

Great lines from this book:

⁕ Ratings ⁕

Plot: 1 2 3 4 5

Characters: 1 2 3 4 5

Ease of reading: 1 2 3 4 5

Overall

☹ 😐 ☺

80

Paperback ○ Hardback ○ e-book ○ Spoken word ○

Title:

Dates

Started: ____________

Finished: ____________

Source

Bought ○ Loaned ○

From: ____________

Author: ____________

Cover picture: ____________

Page count: ____________

○ Fiction

Type: ____________

○ Non-fiction

Subject: ____________

Inspiration Tree

Why I read it?

____

It inspired me to (read/learn/visit)?

____

____

Who will I recommend it to?

____

My Review: ____________

✻ Ratings ✻

Plot: 1 2 3 4 5

Characters:

1 2 3 4 5

Ease of reading:

1 2 3 4 5

Overall

☹ 😐 ☺

Great lines from this book:

Paperback ○ Hardback ○ e-book ○ Spoken word ○

Title:

81

Author:

Cover picture:

Page count:

○ Fiction

Type:

○ Non-fiction

Subject:

Dates

Started:

Finished:

Source

Bought ○ Loaned ○

From:

My Review:

Inspiration Tree

Why I read it?

It inspired me to (read/learn/visit)?

Who will I recommend it to?

Great lines from this book:

⁂ Ratings ⁂

Plot: 1 2 3 4 5

Characters: 1 2 3 4 5

Ease of reading: 1 2 3 4 5

Overall

82

Paperback ○ Hardback ○ e-book ○ Spoken word ○

Title:

Dates

Started: ____________

Finished: __________

Source

Bought ○ Loaned ○

From: ______________

Author: ______________________________

Cover picture: ______________________________

Page count: ______________

○ Fiction

Type: ______________

○ Non-fiction

Subject: ______________

Inspiration Tree

Why I read it?

____

It inspired me to (read/learn/visit)?

____

____

Who will I recommend it to?

____

My Review: ______________________________

⁕ Ratings ⁕

Plot: 1 2 3 4 5

Characters: 1 2 3 4 5

Ease of reading: 1 2 3 4 5

Overall

☹ 😐 ☺

Great lines from this book:

Paperback ○ Hardback ○ e-book ○ Spoken word ○

Title:

83

Author:

Cover picture:

Page count:

○ Fiction

Type:

○ Non-fiction

Subject:

Dates

Started:

Finished:

Source

Bought ○ Loaned ○

From:

My Review:

Inspiration Tree

Why I read it?

It inspired me to (read/learn/visit)?

Who will I recommend it to?

⋇ Ratings ⋇

Plot: 1 2 3 4 5

Characters:

1 2 3 4 5

Ease of reading:

1 2 3 4 5

Overall

Great lines from this book:

84

Paperback ○ Hardback ○ e-book ○ Spoken word ○

Title:

Dates

Started: ____________

Finished: ____________

Source

Bought ○ Loaned ○

From: ____________

Author: ____________

Cover picture: ____________

Page count: ____________

○ Fiction

Type: ____________

○ Non-fiction

Subject: ____________

Inspiration Tree

Why I read it?

____

It inspired me to (read/learn/visit)?

____

____

Who will I recommend it to?

____

My Review: ____________

✱ Ratings ✱

Plot: 1 2 3 4 5

Characters: 1 2 3 4 5

Ease of reading: 1 2 3 4 5

Overall

☹ 😐 ☺

Great lines from this book:

Paperback ○ Hardback ○ e-book ○ Spoken word ○

Title:

85

Author:

Cover picture:

Page count:

○ Fiction

Type:

○ Non-fiction

Subject:

Dates

Started:

Finished:

Source

Bought ○ Loaned ○

From:

My Review:

Inspiration Tree

Why I read it?

It inspired me to (read/learn/visit)?

Who will I recommend it to?

⁎ Ratings ⁎

Plot: 1 2 3 4 5

Characters: 1 2 3 4 5

Ease of reading: 1 2 3 4 5

Overall

Great lines from this book:

86

Paperback ○ Hardback ○ e-book ○ Spoken word ○

Title:

Dates

Started: ____________

Finished: ____________

Source

Bought ○ Loaned ○

From: ____________

Author: ____________

Cover picture: ____________

Page count: ____________

○ Fiction

Type: ____________

○ Non-fiction

Subject: ____________

Inspiration Tree

Why I read it?

____

It inspired me to (read/learn/visit)?

____

____

Who will I recommend it to?

____

My Review: ____________

✱ Ratings ✱

Plot: 1 2 3 4 5

Characters: 1 2 3 4 5

Ease of reading: 1 2 3 4 5

Overall

Great lines from this book:

Paperback ○ Hardback ○ e-book ○ Spoken word ○

Title:

87

Author:

Cover picture:

Page count:

○ Fiction

Type:

○ Non-fiction

Subject:

Dates

Started:

Finished:

Source

Bought ○ Loaned ○

From:

My Review:

Inspiration Tree

Why I read it?

It inspired me to (read/learn/visit)?

Who will I recommend it to?

Great lines from this book:

* Ratings *

Plot: 1 2 3 4 5

Characters: 1 2 3 4 5

Ease of reading: 1 2 3 4 5

Overall

88

Paperback ○ Hardback ○ e-book ○ Spoken word ○

Title:

Dates

Started: ___________

Finished: ___________

Source

Bought ○ Loaned ○

From: ___________

Author: ___________

Cover picture: ___________

Page count: ___________

○ Fiction

Type: ___________

○ Non-fiction

Subject: ___________

My Review: ___________

Inspiration Tree

Why I read it?

It inspired me to (read/learn/visit)?

Who will I recommend it to?

⁎ Ratings ⁎

Plot: 1 2 3 4 5

Characters: 1 2 3 4 5

Ease of reading: 1 2 3 4 5

Overall

Great lines from this book:

Paperback ○ Hardback ○ e-book ○ Spoken word ○

89

Title:

Author:

Cover picture:

Page count:

○ Fiction

Type:

○ Non-fiction

Subject:

My Review:

Great lines from this book:

Dates

Started:

Finished:

Source

Bought ○ Loaned ○

From:

Inspiration Tree

Why I read it?

It inspired me to (read/learn/visit)?

Who will I recommend it to?

⁂ Ratings ⁂

Plot: 1 2 3 4 5

Characters:

1 2 3 4 5

Ease of reading:

1 2 3 4 5

Overall

90

Paperback ○ Hardback ○ e-book ○ Spoken word ○

Title:

Dates

Started: ___________

Finished: _________

Source

Bought ○ Loaned ○

From: ______________

Author: ____________________

Cover picture: ____________________

Page count: ______________

○ Fiction

Type: ______________

○ Non-fiction

Subject: ______________

Inspiration Tree

Why I read it?

____

It inspired me to (read/learn/visit)?

____

____

Who will I recommend it to?

____

My Review: ____________________

✳ Ratings ✳

Plot: 1 2 3 4 5

Characters: 1 2 3 4 5

Ease of reading: 1 2 3 4 5

Overall

Great lines from this book:

Paperback ○ Hardback ○ e-book ○ Spoken word ○

91

Title:

Author: ______

Cover picture: ______

Page count: ______

○ Fiction

Type: ______

○ Non-fiction

Subject: ______

My Review: ______

Great lines from this book:

Dates

Started: ______

Finished: ______

Source

Bought ○ Loaned ○

From: ______

Inspiration Tree

Why I read it?

______

It inspired me to (read/learn/visit)?

______

______

Who will I recommend it to?

______

⁎ Ratings ⁎

Plot: 1 2 3 4 5

Characters: 1 2 3 4 5

Ease of reading: 1 2 3 4 5

Overall

92

Paperback ○ Hardback ○ e-book ○ Spoken word ○

Title:

Dates

Started: ______

Finished: ______

Source

Bought ○ Loaned ○

From: ______

Author: ______

Cover picture: ______

Page count: ______

○ Fiction

Type: ______

○ Non-fiction

Subject: ______

My Review: ______

Inspiration Tree

Why I read it?

______

It inspired me to (read/learn/visit)?

______

Who will I recommend it to?

______

⁕ Ratings ⁕

Plot: 1 2 3 4 5

Characters: 1 2 3 4 5

Ease of reading: 1 2 3 4 5

Overall

☹ 😐 ☺

Great lines from this book:

Paperback ○ Hardback ○ e-book ○ Spoken word ○

Title:

93

Author:

Cover picture:

Page count:

○ Fiction

Type:

○ Non-fiction

Subject:

Dates

Started:

Finished:

Source

Bought ○ Loaned ○

From:

My Review:

Inspiration Tree

Why I read it?

It inspired me to (read/learn/visit)?

Who will I recommend it to?

Great lines from this book:

✳ Ratings ✳

Plot: 1 2 3 4 5

Characters: 1 2 3 4 5

Ease of reading: 1 2 3 4 5

Overall

☹ 😐 ☺

94

Paperback ○ Hardback ○ e-book ○ Spoken word ○

Title:

Dates

Started: ____________

Finished: ____________

Source

Bought ○ Loaned ○

From: ____________

Author: ____________

Cover picture: ____________

Page count: ____________

○ Fiction

Type: ____________

○ Non-fiction

Subject: ____________

My Review: ____________

Inspiration Tree

Why I read it?

____

It inspired me to (read/learn/visit)?

____

____

Who will I recommend it to?

____

⁎ Ratings ⁎

Plot: 1 2 3 4 5

Characters: 1 2 3 4 5

Ease of reading: 1 2 3 4 5

Overall

☹ 😐 ☺

Great lines from this book:

Paperback ○ Hardback ○ e-book ○ Spoken word ○

Title:

95

Author:

Cover picture:

Page count:

○ Fiction
Type:

○ Non-fiction
Subject:

Dates
Started:
Finished:

Source
Bought ○ Loaned ○
From:

My Review:

Inspiration Tree

Why I read it?

It inspired me to (read/learn/visit)?

Who will I recommend it to?

Great lines from this book:

⁕ Ratings ⁕

Plot: 1 2 3 4 5

Characters:
1 2 3 4 5

Ease of reading:
1 2 3 4 5

Overall
☹ 😐 ☺

96

Paperback ○ Hardback ○ e-book ○ Spoken word ○

Title:

Dates

Started: ____________

Finished: ____________

Source

Bought ○ Loaned ○

From: ____________

Author: ____________

Cover picture: ____________

Page count: ____________

○ Fiction

Type: ____________

○ Non-fiction

Subject: ____________

Inspiration Tree

Why I read it?

____

It inspired me to (read/learn/visit)?

____

____

Who will I recommend it to?

____

My Review: ____________

✳ Ratings ✳

Plot: 1 2 3 4 5

Characters: 1 2 3 4 5

Ease of reading: 1 2 3 4 5

Overall

Great lines from this book:

Paperback ○ Hardback ○ e-book ○ Spoken word ○

97

Title:

Author:

Cover picture:

Page count:

○ Fiction

Type:

○ Non-fiction

Subject:

Dates

Started:

Finished:

Source

Bought ○ Loaned ○

From:

My Review:

Inspiration Tree

Why I read it?

It inspired me to (read/learn/visit)?

Who will I recommend it to?

⁂ Ratings ⁂

Plot: 1 2 3 4 5

Characters: 1 2 3 4 5

Ease of reading: 1 2 3 4 5

Overall

Great lines from this book:

98

Paperback ○ Hardback ○ e-book ○ Spoken word ○

Title:

Dates
Started: ________
Finished: ________

Source
Bought ○ Loaned ○
From: ________

Author: ________
Cover picture: ________
Page count: ________

○ Fiction
Type: ________

○ Non-fiction
Subject: ________

Inspiration Tree

Why I read it?

____

It inspired me to (read/learn/visit)?

____

____

Who will I recommend it to?

____

My Review: ________

* Ratings *

Plot: 1 2 3 4 5

Characters:
1 2 3 4 5

Ease of reading:
1 2 3 4 5

Overall

Great lines from this book:

Paperback ○ Hardback ○ e-book ○ Spoken word ○

Title:

99

Author:

Cover picture:

Page count:

○ Fiction
Type:

○ Non-fiction
Subject:

Dates
Started:
Finished:

Source
Bought ○ Loaned ○
From:

My Review:

Inspiration Tree

Why I read it?

It inspired me to (read/learn/visit)?

Who will I recommend it to?

⁂ Ratings ⁂

Plot: 1 2 3 4 5

Characters:
1 2 3 4 5

Ease of reading:
1 2 3 4 5

Overall

☹ 😐 ☺

Great lines from this book:

100

Paperback ○ Hardback ○ e-book ○ Spoken word ○

Title:

Dates

Started: ___________

Finished: ___________

Source

Bought ○ Loaned ○

From: ___________

Inspiration Tree

Why I read it?

____

It inspired me to (read/learn/visit)?

____

____

Who will I recommend it to?

____

✱ Ratings ✱

Plot: 1 2 3 4 5

Characters: 1 2 3 4 5

Ease of reading: 1 2 3 4 5

Overall

☹ 😐 ☺

Author: ___________

Cover picture: ___________

Page count: ___________

○ Fiction

Type: ___________

○ Non-fiction

Subject: ___________

My Review: ___________

Great lines from this book:

The Big Read

Top 100 Voted Fiction Books (Children's in bold)

- 1. The Lord of the Rings, JRR Tolkien
- 2. Pride and Prejudice, Jane Austen
- **3. His Dark Materials, Philip Pullman**
- 4. The Hitchhiker's Guide to the Galaxy, Douglas Adams
- **5. Harry Potter and the Goblet of Fire, JK Rowling**
- 6. To Kill a Mockingbird, Harper Lee
- **7. Winnie the Pooh, AA Milne**
- 8. Nineteen Eighty-Four, George Orwell
- **9. The Lion, the Witch and the Wardrobe, CS Lewis**
- 10. Jane Eyre, Charlotte Brontë
- 11. Catch-22, Joseph Heller
- 12. Wuthering Heights, Emily Brontë
- 13. Birdsong, Sebastian Faulks
- 14. Rebecca, Daphne du Maurier
- 15. The Catcher in the Rye, JD Salinger
- **16. The Wind in the Willows, Kenneth Grahame**
- 17. Great Expectations, Charles Dickens
- 18. Little Women, Louisa May Alcott
- 19. Captain Corelli's Mandolin, Louis de Bernieres
- 20. War and Peace, Leo Tolstoy
- 21. Gone with the Wind, Margaret Mitchell
- **22. Harry Potter And The Philosopher's Stone, JK Rowling**
- **23. Harry Potter And The Chamber Of Secrets, JK Rowling**
- **24. Harry Potter And The Prisoner Of Azkaban, JK Rowling**
- **25. The Hobbit, JRR Tolkien**
- 26. Tess Of The D'Urbervilles, Thomas Hardy
- 27. Middlemarch, George Eliot
- 28. A Prayer For Owen Meany, John Irving
- 29. The Grapes Of Wrath, John Steinbeck
- **30. Alice's Adventures In Wonderland, Lewis Carroll**

- 31. **The Story Of Tracy Beaker, Jacqueline Wilson**
- 32. One Hundred Years Of Solitude, Gabriel García Márquez
- 33. The Pillars Of The Earth, Ken Follett
- 34. David Copperfield, Charles Dickens
- 35. **Charlie And The Chocolate Factory, Roald Dahl**
- 36. **Treasure Island, Robert Louis Stevenson**
- 37. A Town Like Alice, Nevil Shute
- 38. Persuasion, Jane Austen
- 39. Dune, Frank Herbert
- 40. Emma, Jane Austen
- 41. **Anne Of Green Gables, LM Montgomery**
- 42. **Watership Down, Richard Adams**
- 43. The Great Gatsby, F Scott Fitzgerald
- 44. The Count Of Monte Cristo, Alexandre Dumas
- 45. Brideshead Revisited, Evelyn Waugh
- 46. Animal Farm, George Orwell
- 47. A Christmas Carol, Charles Dickens
- 48. Far From The Madding Crowd, Thomas Hardy
- 49. **Goodnight Mister Tom, Michelle Magorian**
- 50. The Shell Seekers, Rosamunde Pilc
- 51. **The Secret Garden, Frances Hodgson Burnett**
- 52. Of Mice And Men, John Steinbeck
- 53. The Stand, Stephen King
- 54. Anna Karenina, Leo Tolstoy
- 55. **A Suitable Boy, Vikram Seth**
- 56. **The BFG, Roald Dahl**
- 57. **Swallows And Amazons, Arthur Ransome**
- 58. **Black Beauty, Anna Sewell**
- 59. **Artemis Fowl, Eoin Colfer**
- 60. Crime And Punishment, Fyodor Dostoyevsky
- 61. **Noughts And Crosses, Malorie Blackman**
- 62. Memoirs Of A Geisha, Arthur Golden
- 63. A Tale Of Two Cities, Charles Dickens
- 64. The Thorn Birds, Colleen McCollough
- 65. Mort, Terry Pratchett

- **66. The Magic Faraway Tree, Enid Blyton**
- 67. The Magus, John Fowles
- 68. Good Omens, Terry Pratchett and Neil Gaiman
- 69. Guards! Guards!, Terry Pratchett
- 70. Lord Of The Flies, William Golding
- 71. Perfume, Patrick Süskind
- 72. The Ragged Trousered Philanthropists, Robert Tressell
- 73. Night Watch, Terry Pratchett
- **74. Matilda, Roald Dahl**
- 75. Bridget Jones's Diary, Helen Fielding
- 76. The Secret History, Donna Tartt
- 77. The Woman In White, Wilkie Collins
- 78. Ulysses, James Joyce
- 79. Bleak House, Charles Dickens
- **80. Double Act, Jacqueline Wilson**
- **81. The Twits, Roald Dahl**
- 82. I Capture The Castle, Dodie Smith
- 83. Holes, Louis Sachar
- 84. Gormenghast, Mervyn Peake
- 85. The God Of Small Things, Arundhati Roy
- **86. Vicky Angel, Jacqueline Wilson**
- 87. Brave New World, Aldous Huxley
- 88. Cold Comfort Farm, Stella Gibbons
- 89. Magician, Raymond E Feist
- 90. On The Road, Jack Kerouac
- 91. The Godfather, Mario Puzo
- 92. The Clan Of The Cave Bear, Jean M Auel
- 93. The Colour Of Magic, Terry Pratchett
- 94. The Alchemist, Paulo Coelho
- 95. Katherine, Anya Seton
- 96. Kane And Abel, Jeffrey Archer
- 97. Love In The Time Of Cholera, Gabriel García Márquez
- **98. Girls In Love, Jacqueline Wilson**
- **99. The Princess Diaries, Meg Cabot**
- 100. Midnight's Children, Salman Rushdie

Notes: (books to read, new authors, reading resources etc.)

Loan Record

Book	Borrowed from	Leant to	Date Borrowed	Date Returned

67689716R00063

Made in the USA
Columbia, SC
31 July 2019